Christmas Tree Decorations

with
Valerie Janitch

Editor
Brenda Ross

Photography
Melvin Grey

Illustrations
Penny Brown

COLNE PROMOTIONS

First published in 1994 by
Colne Promotions
PO Box 420
Colney Heath
St Albans
Herts AL4 0YA

ISBN 1 899539 01 8

Design and pre-press production by John Boulden, Byfleet

Printed by Crowes, Norwich

Contents

Step by step instructions are given for each project, with references where appropriate to specific techniques explained in the basics section at the back of the book.

To make the decorations in this book you require only basic equipment that is available in most homes. All measurements are shown in both metric and imperial. Use one or the other, but do not mix them or compare them; they are worked out independently and whichever you choose you will get a successful result. Where two measurements are stated, such as for a piece of fabric, the depth is given first, followed by the width. Unless otherwise specified, 3mm ($^1/_8$ in) is allowed for seams.

The projects in this book are intended for decorations only and are not suitable as toys for young children.

Stocking sachets

These tiny Christmas stockings can be filled with lavender or pot pourri, to make a fragrant tree decoration. One side of the stocking is fabric, and the other side is felt. Each stocking is approximately 10cm (4in) long.

MATERIALS

For each stocking:

10cm x 9cm (4in x 3½in) piece of medium-weight cotton fabric.

Two pieces of toning felt – one piece 10cm x 9cm (4in x 3½in), for one side of the stocking, and the other piece 3cm x 6cm (1¼in x 2½in), for the cuff at the top of the stocking.

30cm (12in) of 1cm (³⁄₈in) wide lace.

15cm (6in) of narrow ribbon – about 5mm (¼in) wide.

30cm (12in) of gold gauze gift-tie, 4cm (1½in) wide.

15cm (6in) of fine gold cord or thick crochet cotton.

Matching sewing threads.

Lavender or pot pourri to fill.

Clear adhesive.

STOCKING PATTERN

1 *Trace this pattern and cut it out.*

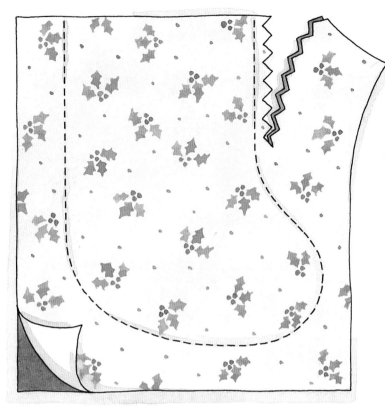

2 Place the fabric right side up on the larger piece of felt, and pin the pattern on top, placing the top edge of the pattern level with the edge of the fabric and felt. Using thread to match the felt, stitch neatly all round the edge of the pattern. Then remove the pattern and cut approximately 5mm (¼in) outside the stitching line with pinking shears.

3 Lightly fill the stocking with lavender or pot pourri – too much will spoil the shape – and tack the edges together across the top. Fold the strip of felt in half lengthways and place the fold over the top of the stocking, to form a cuff on each side of the stocking. Slipstitch the long edges to the front and back of the stocking, and oversew together the sides of the felt.

4 Stitch two rows of lace all round the cuff, with the straight edges meeting at the centre and the outer edges jutting beyond the edges of the cuff.

5 Glue the narrow ribbon over the stitching lines. Then knot the cut ends of the cord to form a loop and sew the knot to the back of the stocking.

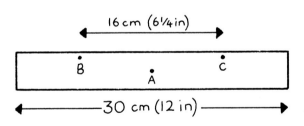

6 Make the gauze gift-tie into a butterfly bow as in basics section 3, but position point A in the centre of the ribbon instead of at the edge, as shown here. Glue the bow to the stocking, pinching it over the top back corner.

Mini crackers

Tiny crackers,
11cm (4½in) long,
make a pretty tree trim.

1 *Cracker making is not difficult; the secret lies in a pair of formers (shapes round which the crackers are formed). To make the formers for these miniature crackers, cut a 2cm (³/₄ in) diameter hole in a piece of thin card.*

2 *Roll up a 12cm (4³/₄ in) square of medium-weight white paper and fit it in the hole, allowing it to open out so that it fits snugly against the side. Check that the cut edges at each end of the tube are level, then tape the overlap and remove the tube. Roll up some waste paper and pack it into the tube, making it firm and solid. Make a second former in exactly the same way, but only 8cm (3in) long.*

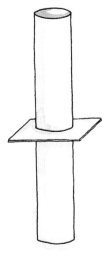

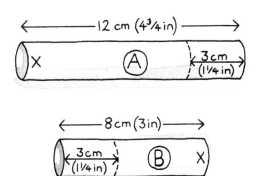

3 *Mark the larger former A and the smaller former B, and draw a line round each former 3cm (1¹/₄ in) from one end, as shown by the broken lines here. This end becomes the inner end. Indicate the outer ends with an X.*

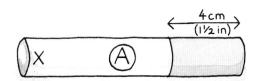

4 *Cut a 4cm x 14cm (1¹/₂in x 5¹/₂in) strip of white paper (shown here in cream) and roll it smoothly round the longer tube, level with the inner end. Tape the overlap.*

MATERIALS

Coloured crêpe paper.

Medium-weight white paper – for formers and lining.

Waste paper (not too thick – magazines etc) – for formers.

Thin card – for template.

35cm (³/₈yd) of lace, about 1.5cm (⁵/₈in) deep – for trimming.

50cm (¹/₂yd) of curling ribbon (gift-tie) – for decoration.

15cm (6in) of 7mm (¹/₄in) wide single-face satin ribbon – for roses.

Sewing thread to match the crêpe paper – for tying the crackers.

Green or black sewing threads – for hanging the crackers.

Double-sided tape.

Clear adhesive.

Mini crackers

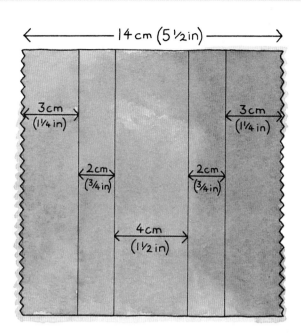

5 Prepare a 14cm (5½in) square of crêpe paper, cutting the two edges that cross the grain with pinking shears. Rule vertical lines parallel with the pinked edges, spaced according to the measurements shown here. The grain will be running in the direction of the horizontal arrows shown.

14 cm (5½in)

3cm (1¼in)   2cm (¾in)   4cm (1½in)   2cm (¾in)   3cm (1¼in)

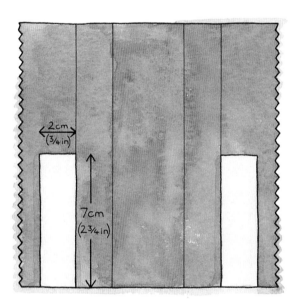

2cm (¾in)

7cm (2¾in)

6 Cut two 7cm x 2cm (2¾in x ¾in) strips of white paper and fix them to the crêpe paper as shown here, using double-sided tape. These become the linings of the ends of the crackers.

7 Place tube A on the crêpe paper with the strip of white paper matching the two inner lines on the crêpe paper as shown. Tape the paper roll to the edge of the crêpe paper, where it touches the crêpe.

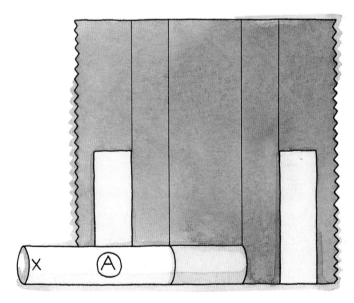

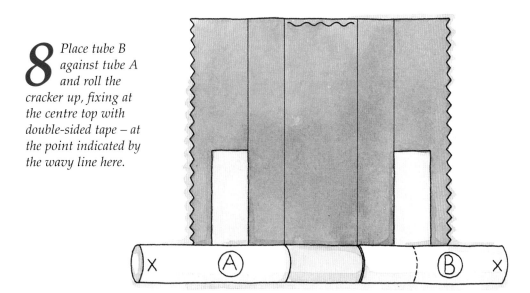

8 *Place tube B against tube A and roll the cracker up, fixing at the centre top with double-sided tape – at the point indicated by the wavy line here.*

9 *Draw out tube B as far as the outer marked line on the crêpe paper, then wind matching thread twice round the shaded area shown here, draw it up tight, and knot securely. Remove the tube.*

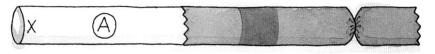

10 *Draw out tube A as far as the outer marked line, leaving the paper roll – which you taped to the crêpe paper – in the cracker, and tie round the shaded area as described above.*

11 *Gently stretch the crêpe paper at each end between the fingertips, to frill the edges. Separate the two layers to make a double frill.*

12 *Glue lace around each end. Mark the centre of the curling ribbon, then cut or tear it into very narrow strips from each end, leaving about 4cm (1½in) at the centre. Tie the centre around the cracker, knotting tightly underneath. Draw the lengths of ribbon between your thumb and the blade of a knife or scissors until they are tightly curled.*

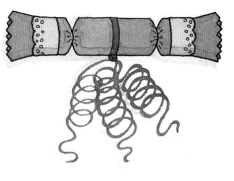

13 *Glue the cut ends of a 15cm (6in) length of lace together to form a circle. Gather the straight edge and draw up into a rosette with a small hole in the centre. Glue to the centre of the cracker, over the curling ribbon, just above the knot of the ribbon. Then make a ribbon rose (see basics section 1) and glue it in the centre of the rosette. Alternatively, trim the cracker with a butterfly bow (see basics section 3).*

14 *Fix a loop of green or black thread through the curling ribbon that is round the cracker, to hang the cracker from a branch.*

Roly-poly snowmen

1 Fold a sheet of waste paper in half and open it out again. Push a skewer or knitting needle into one of the balls so that it is firmly held. Spread the ball thickly with PVA adhesive, and holding it over the waste paper sprinkle glitter liberally all over the wet surface. Pat the glitter into the adhesive gently, tap the ball to shake off the excess and allow it to dry. Meanwhile carefully tip the excess glitter back into the tube and cover the second ball in the same way.

Snowmen with the frosty sparkle of snowballs brighten up the tree with their cheerful grins and colourful scarves. They are each approximately 8cm (3in) tall and 4cm (1½in) wide at the widest point of the body.

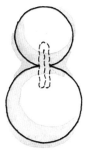

2 Bend the craft stem or pipe cleaner in half and glue it into both balls, to join them together, as shown here.

MATERIALS
For each snowman:

Two turned paper balls – one 3cm (1¼in) in diameter for the head, and the other 4cm (1½in) in diameter for the body.

20cm (8in) of 1cm (³⁄₈in) wide ribbon – for the scarf.

Black and green medium-weight paper – for the hat and holly leaves.

Small wooden bead about 5mm (¼in) in diameter – for the nose.

Two tiny black beads – for the eyes.

A few tiny red beads – for the holly berries.

15cm (6in) of crochet cotton or thick black thread – for the hanging loop.

5cm (2in) craft stem or pipe cleaner.

Tube of white glitter powder.

Black rollerball pen.

PVA adhesive.

Clear adhesive (optional).

Skewer or knitting needle.

3 To make the scarf, cut the ribbon into two equal pieces. Unravel both ends of one piece to form a fringe, and place it on the front of the snowman, almost vertical, as shown here. Glue one end of the second piece of ribbon at right angles over the first piece, level with the head/body join. Wrap it closely round the neck and glue the other end on top, trimming off the surplus. Fold down the top part of the first piece of ribbon, twisting it if it has a pattern printed on one side only so that the pattern is facing the front. Glue this piece down over the ribbon round the 'neck'.

4 Cut the hat brim, side and crown once each in black paper, using these patterns.

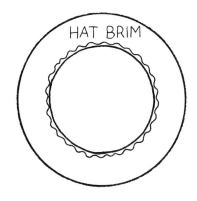

HAT SIDE · OVERLAP

HAT BRIM

HAT CROWN

5 Make the crochet cotton into a loop and thread it through the centre of the crown, marked by the dot on the pattern, knotting the ends together underneath.

6 On the underside of the brim run a trail of glue close to the inner edge, shown by the wavy line on the pattern, and press it firmly down over the head. Curve the hat side round to make a loop and glue the overlap. Run glue inside the lower edge of the hat side, shown by the wavy line on the pattern, and press it down over the brim. Run glue all round close to the edge underneath the crown, shown by the wavy line on the pattern, then press it down on top of the hat side. When the hat is completely dry, trim off the slight overlap of the crown, level with the side.

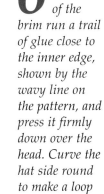

7 Glue the nose into place using tweezers. Use a pin to position the eyes, with a spot of glue on the end of the pin as shown above. Draw a curved line for the mouth.

8 Cut three holly leaves in green paper using this pattern, and glue them to the hat, adding a cluster of tiny red beads at the centre.

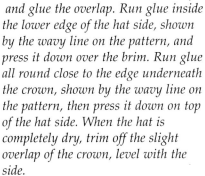

Victorian candy cones

Sugared almonds in little covered paper cones were a favourite 19th century Christmas tree decoration. These two interpretations are typical of the period: a traditional Christmas design, and a variation that is pure romantic Victoriana. Choose paper, fabric and trimming to match your theme.

Each cone is about 12cm (5in) long, and approximately 6cm (2½ in) wide at its widest point.

MATERIALS

For each cone:

Medium-weight plain paper.

Gift-wrap paper to cover.

6cm x 17cm (2½in x 7in) of medium-weight cotton fabric.

50cm (½yd) of 1.5mm (¹⁄₁₆in) wide satin ribbon.

Matching thread.

Adhesive tape.

Clear adhesive.

In addition, for traditional Christmas version:

20cm (¼yd) of velvet tubing ribbon.

Christmas motif.

In addition, for romantic version:

75cm (¾yd) of 1.5mm (¹⁄₁₆in) wide satin ribbon.

70cm (¾yd) of 1cm (³⁄₈in) wide lace.

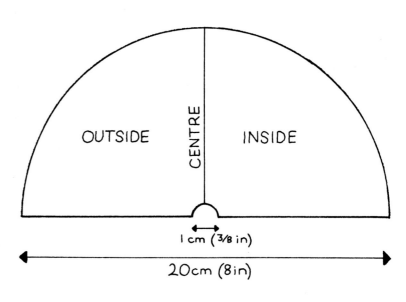

1 Draw a semi-circle on the plain paper as shown here, using a base line of 20cm (8in). Mark the centre line.

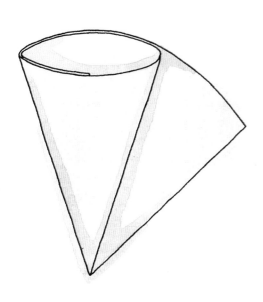

2 Cut it out and curve it round to form a cone of double paper, matching one edge of the paper exactly to the centre line and keeping the curved edges level. Tape the join. Cut a similar piece of gift-wrap and curve it smoothly round the cone. Glue the overlap.

3 Join the short edges of the fabric to form a circle, right side inside, and press the seam open.

4 Turn the top edge of the fabric tube over 1cm ($^1/_2$in) and stitch 5mm ($^1/_4$in) below the fold to form a channel for the drawstrings. Turn up the lower edge about 3mm ($^1/_8$in) and tack.

6 Gently pull the fabric tube up, turning it right side out. Make a small slit in the channel at each side. Cut the ribbon into two pieces and thread one piece through each slit right round the channel. Overlap and stitch the cut ends of each drawstring, so that they are securely joined.

5 Turn the fabric tube upside down and fit it over the cone, right sides facing, then oversew the edge of the tube and the top edge of the cone together.

7 **Christmas cone** – to trim, glue the velvet tubing around the top edge, and stick a cut-out motif to the cone, such as a suitable motif cut from a greetings card or Christmas wrapping paper.

8 **Romantic cone** – to trim, cut the lace into two equal pieces, overlap the straight edges and gather. Draw up the lace to fit round the top of the cone and glue it in place, distributing the gathers evenly. Plait the ribbon to make braid (see basics section 2) and glue it over the gathers of the lace.

Victorian baubles

Round the top half, eight vertical stripes of braid match the colour of the egg; similar stripes of 3mm (1/8in) wide ribbon go around the lower section. All the interest is around the centre: a band of black lace topped with green braid; alternate pink and cream miniature roses made from 3mm (1/8in) wide ribbon (see basics section 1); pearls between the roses. The large pearl holding the loop at the top is surrounded by two circles of pink-tinted pearls. Two smaller pearls decorate the bottom of the bauble.

Six stripes of green braid, matching the colour of the bauble, alternate with a very narrow silver trimming. Mother-of-pearl flower sequins on the braid are centred with tiny pearls, and there are arrangements of the same pearls in graduated sizes at the top and bottom of the bauble.

Divided into four with a dainty, embroidered flower trimming in pink, yellow and brown, each quarter is then decorated with two stripes of 3mm (1/8in) wide gold lurex ribbon, and one stripe of plaited braid (see basics section 2) in matching pink and brown, using a double length of pink and a single length of brown. Small, dark brown wooden beads make the top and bottom decoration, with small gold beads that emphasise the gold lurex trimming.

These decorations look so romantic, but their contents are more down to earth: cook a couple of tasty omelettes before you start work – and use the egg shells for these baubles. They are so enjoyable to make that as soon as you have finished those you will be dashing off to the shops to buy another carton of eggs. But as you will be feeding the family too, you need not feel guilty!

MATERIALS

Hen's eggs – the ones used here were size 2.

Coloured soft-ply tissue: table napkins, face tissues, toilet tissue etc – for the papier mâché covering.

Oddments of ribbon, braid, lace, gift-tie and other trimming.

Assorted beads – for trimming and to hold hanging loops.

Crochet cotton, fine cord or strong sewing thread – for hanging loops.

Fine sandpaper – for smoothing the papier mâché.

Linseed oil – for surface finishing.

Paper towel, soft rag or tissue – for applying the oil.

Wallpaper paste – for papier mâché.

Clear adhesive – for applying decoration.

A band of delicate blue and white lace runs round the middle, with a band of fancy guipure lace over the top edge and a row of blue-tinted pearls immediately above that. A small circle of the same pearls at the top is surrounded by some narrow white braid and another guipure lace. On the bottom section are white guipure daisies. A single blue daisy on the bottom of the bauble holds a small blue bead with a blue pearl underneath.

Four vertical stripes of highly decorative braid to match the colour of the bauble are balanced in between by stripes of very narrow folded cream lace. At the centre of each segment is a lemon yellow rose (see basics section 1) made from 7mm (¼in) wide ribbon, with a leafy cluster above and below. To make this cluster, form a knot close to the end of a 3mm (⅛in) wide piece of leaf green ribbon; glue the cut end underneath and trim off the excess, then glue the other end underneath in the same way. Apply the leaf cluster to the bauble with tweezers. At the top of the egg two circles of tiny pearls surround one large pearl, and there is just one tiny pearl at the bottom.

Eight vertical strands of gold lurex crochet cotton are glued at even intervals round the egg, from top to bottom. Shorter strands divide alternate segments round the top half, and the same on the bottom half in the opposite four segments. A band of cream braid round the middle is centred with a string of tiny pearls. Embroidered floral motifs are glued into the remaining undivided sections. A large blue wooden bead at the top holds a loop of the same gold lurex crochet cotton, and is surrounded by a ring of small blue wooden beads. At the bottom a small blue wooden bead has a minute gold bead underneath.

1 *First blow the eggs (see basics section 4). When they are quite drained and dry, cover them with coloured tissue papier mâché. To do this you will need only a small amount of soft tissue, such as less than half a paper napkin, one face tissue, or a couple of sheets of toilet tissue. Watch out for pretty tissues on a friend's dressing table, a lovely deep coloured napkin in a restaurant, or a suitable shade of toilet tissue in the ladies room! Cut the tissue into tiny pieces – roughly 1.5cm to 2cm (½in to ¾in) square – but do not worry too much about the size. Carefully separate the layers of tissue so that they are all single-ply.*

2 *Make up a small amount of wallpaper paste and liberally paste half the egg; I use a 2cm (¾in) wide paint brush as a pasting brush. Then begin covering the egg with a layer of tissue, overlapping the edges so that there are no gaps; use the brush to pick up the tiny pieces of tissue, and brush more paste over them once they are in position. Paste the rest of the egg and continue until there is a complete layer of tissue covering the shell, all the time brushing on more paste so that the paper is saturated. Add several more layers of tissue in the same way, so that the egg is evenly covered.*

Victorian baubles

3 *Leave the egg in a warm place to dry, resting it on a plastic bag and turning it several times so that it dries all over. A window sill in the sun is the best drying place, but the paper covering needs to dry really hard, so it is a good idea to finish the eggs off in the bottom of a cool oven.*

4 *Carefully sandpaper the egg all over, so that any wrinkles are smoothed out. Then pour a little oil on to a plate. I use linseed oil, but olive oil or any clear, good, cooking oil will do. Wipe the paper towel or rag over the plate so that the oil is thoroughly absorbed, then very gently smooth it over the egg so that just a little of the oil is absorbed, giving it a slight sheen and intensifying the colour. Take care because it is easy to darken the colour too much; go carefully, continuing to rub the oil in until you have just the depth of colour you want.*

5 *Now for the really interesting part – decorating the bauble. Working with the pointed end of the egg at the bottom, glue on odd bits of lace, braid, ribbons, sequins, feathers, tiny tassels or anything else you have. Try making plaited braid (see basics section 2), ribbon roses (basics section 1) or butterfly bows (basics section 3), and add strings of bead trimming or single beads. Tweezers and a pin are invaluable at this stage; apply a tiny blob of glue to the surface of the bead, or the point of the pin, and allow it to set slightly before pressing the bead into position. See panel below for more on decoration.*

6 *When you have finished the decoration of your bauble, glue beads at top and bottom, as on the baubles shown, and add a central bead at the top holding a loop of crochet cotton or equivalent, with which to hang the decoration. To form this loop, cut a 15cm (6in) length of crochet cotton and make a knot at each end (a). Pass a needle and thread through the bead, round the middle of the crochet cotton, and back through the bead (b). Pull the needle and both ends of the thread through the bead, and the crochet cotton will follow (c). Glue the knots and base of the bead (d) and press them down on to the centre top of the egg.*

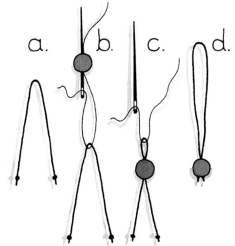

Ideas for decoration

Follow the ideas for decoration shown on these pages, or try some of your own. Designing the decoration of these baubles becomes more fascinating the more you make, because new possibilities and new ways of using oddments of trimming keep emerging. You can, of course, be as bold and brash as you like, but I prefer to try and achieve a more restrained, Victorian effect.

If you too have this image in mind, try not to stray too far from the original base colour, and avoid more than one direct contrast. For instance, of the eggs shown, the one with the most contrast is the brown egg. This needed considerable brightening-up because it was basically so dark, drab and uninteresting. But even so I chose yellow and pink, which are both the same side of the colour spectrum and, if mixed together with a touch of black added, would produce brown. So look out for several different shades of the same basic colour as the egg, or contrasts which have the base colour in them. For example: green, which is a mixture of blue and yellow, on gold; or orange, a mixture of yellow and red, on scarlet.

This more elegant Victorian theme makes a tasteful and refreshing change from the customary mix of bright red and emerald green, which tends to overwhelm everything at Christmas time.

Bears in bags

These miniature carrier bags are around 8cm (3in) high, including the tiny bears and parcels sticking out the top. To make them I used dolls house wallpaper, but any plain or patterned paper will do as long as it is thick enough – about the weight of a good quality writing paper (see supplier section) or cartridge paper.

MATERIALS

For each bag and bear:

Good quality medium-weight coloured paper – for carrier bag.

Gift-wrap paper, not too thick – for parcel.

Thin card – for parcel.

Stiff paper – for making pompons.

Face tissue – for filling the bag.

Narrow gift-tie ribbon, such as curling ribbon, or cut standard ribbon in half – for bag handles.

Gift-tie string or crochet cotton etc – for tying the parcel.

12-15 strands, 76cm (30in) long, of Twilleys stranded embroidery wool, or fine knitting yarn – for the bear; or use purchased pompons: one 3cm (1¼in) in diameter and two 12mm (½in) in diameter.

Scrap of matching felt – for bear's ears.

One tiny black bead and two very tiny black beads – for bear's nose and eyes.

7-8cm (3in) of single-face satin ribbon, 7mm (¼in) wide, for bow on the bear .

Real or artificial greenery – for decoration.

Sewing thread to match ribbon, and black thread for hanging loop.

Adhesive tape.

Glue stick (optional).

Clear adhesive.

Bears in bags

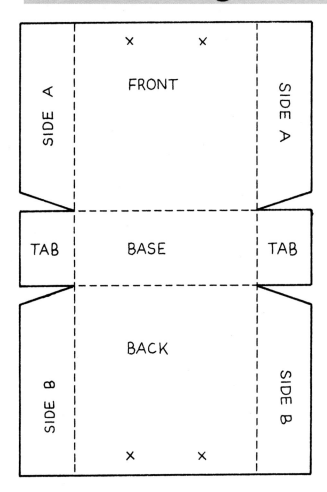

1 Trace this pattern on to the back of the coloured or patterned paper (basics section 5) and cut it out. Score the broken lines.

2 Fold the paper round into shape: fold the base tabs up and glue sides A over them, then bring sides B round and glue in place from top to bottom.

3 Cut two 6cm (2$\frac{1}{2}$in) lengths of gift-tie ribbon and glue the cut ends to the inside of the bag 2cm ($\frac{3}{4}$in) apart, at the points marked X on the pattern, to form the handles. Find the middle of the face tissue and push it down into the bottom of the bag; crumple the remainder as you tuck it down on top, leaving just a little visible above the edge of the bag.

4 To make the parcel, trace the sides pattern once on to thin card (basics section 5), and the end pattern twice. Cut out and score the broken lines.

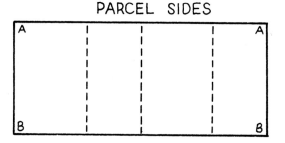

PARCEL SIDES

5 Fold the sides piece round so that A-A and B-B meet; tape the corner join. Then tape the two ends into place. Cut a 5.5cm x 10cm (2$\frac{1}{4}$in x 4in) piece of gift-wrap paper and wrap it neatly round the parcel, gluing it into place. Tie with gift-tie string or crochet cotton.

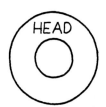

HEAD

PAW

6 To make pompons for the bear's head and paws, trace this head pattern twice and the paw pattern four times on to fairly stiff paper, or draw circles with compasses. Cut out the shapes, cutting away the inner circle.

7 To make the head, separate three strands of wool then place them together again, and thread them into a tapestry needle. Put the two larger circles of paper together and wrap the wool over and over them through the centre hole, as shown here, continuing with more wool until the

centre hole is tight full, as shown above right. Push pointed scissors through the yarn between the edges of the paper circles, and cut through the yarn all round, keeping the scissors between the paper. Slip a length of yarn between the circles to surround the yarn in the centre, and knot it together, pulling tight. Then cut the paper and pull it away.

8 Trim the pompon severely to make a neat, round, firm ball. Repeat the whole process twice more, with two of the smaller paper circles, to make the paws, working with only two strands of wool. Alternatively, if you find this too fiddly, you could cut 12mm (1/2in) diameter circles of felt instead.

9 Cut the ear twice in felt. Part the strands of wool where you plan to have the ears on the head, then glue the ears into place, poking them well in.

10 Glue the nose bead, sideways on, to the centre of the face, and glue the two very tiny beads, for eyes, one at each side with the hole against the face. Glue the paws underneath the face, as shown in the photograph.

11 To assemble the decoration, glue the parcel at one side of the bag and the bear at the other, tucking them down into the tissue as in the photograph. Add a sprig of fresh, dried or artificial greenery in the corner behind the parcel. Make a butterfly bow (basics section 3) from the satin ribbon and glue it to the side of the bear's head, over the corner of the bag, as shown here.

12 Loop a 25cm (10in) length of thread under the handles, for hanging the decoration on the tree.

Lattice hearts

These lattice hearts are made by weaving together two pieces of paper. Accurate measuring is vital for a professional result, but instead of laboriously measuring the lines to cut the shape, use squared paper – a stationery graph pad or child's exercise book.

The size of the squares determines the size of the heart; my squares were 5mm ($^3/_{16}$in), making a heart just over 9cm ($3^1/_2$in) across at the widest point and approximately 9cm ($3^1/_2$in) deep. The squared paper is stuck on the back of the coloured paper, and covered up by the backing.

A good quality writing paper is ideal for making these hearts (see suppliers section at the back of the book). Choose one colour or two, backed with a lighter shade.

MATERIALS

Medium-weight coloured papers.

Squared paper.

Glue stick.

30cm (12in) of very narrow satin ribbon – for each heart.

Pair of compasses.

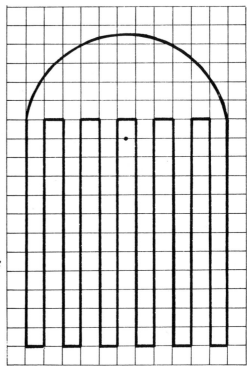

The backing covers up the squared paper.

1 Draw the shape shown here twice on the squared paper; the dot marks the position of the point of the compasses to draw the curve. Cut out leaving one square all round, as shown here. Stick each shape to the back of the coloured paper.

2 *Cut out both pieces, following the ruled lines very carefully.*

3 *Weave the two pieces together at right angles, to form the heart.*

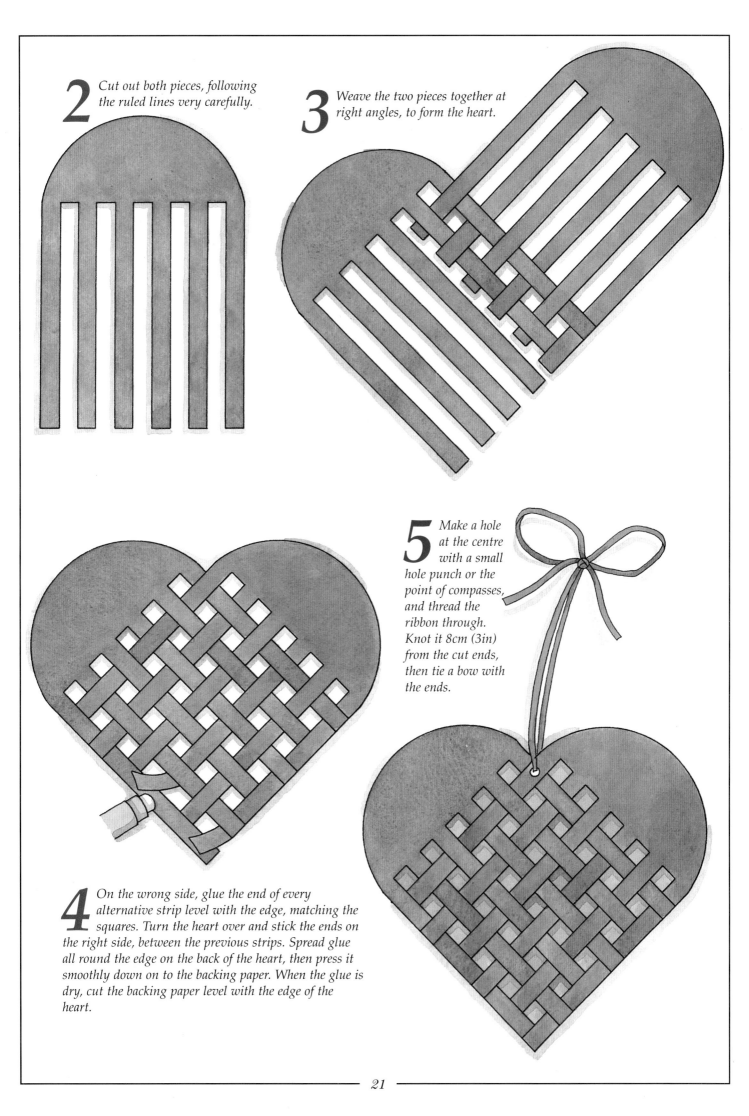

5 *Make a hole at the centre with a small hole punch or the point of compasses, and thread the ribbon through. Knot it 8cm (3in) from the cut ends, then tie a bow with the ends.*

4 *On the wrong side, glue the end of every alternative strip level with the edge, matching the squares. Turn the heart over and stick the ends on the right side, between the previous strips. Spread glue all round the edge on the back of the heart, then press it smoothly down on to the backing paper. When the glue is dry, cut the backing paper level with the edge of the heart.*

Lattice hearts *variation*

See-through heart

For a see-through heart, with no backing, you will need a stiffer paper, or thin card. I stuck two shades of writing paper together, with a plain piece sandwiched between.

6 Draw two shapes on squared paper as in step 1, but allow two squares all round instead of one. Run glue all round the edge on the back of each piece, outside the shape that you will be cutting out. Press the pieces smoothly on to the coloured paper.

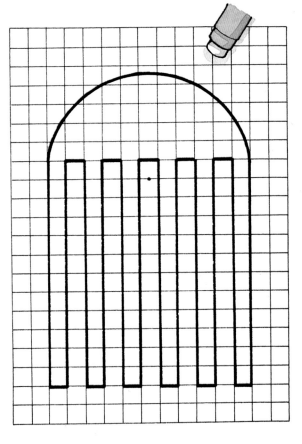

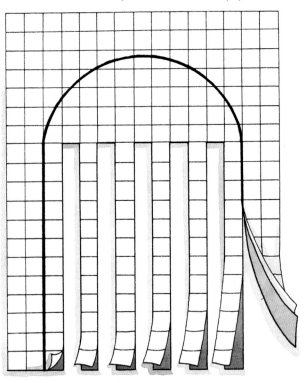

7 Cut away the straight lower edge on each piece, then cut away all the inner sections. Finally cut round the outer edge of the heart, ie inside where the squared paper was glued, and the squared paper will fall away.

8 Weave the two pieces together at right angles, as in step 3, then finish off as in step 4, but take care to space the strips evenly when gluing the ends, as there are no squares for guidance. Finish with ribbon to hang, as in step 5.

Dumpy angel

This plump little angel – just 7cm (2¾in) tall – has a sweet smile that could be angelic – or slightly mischievous.

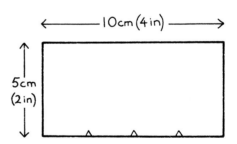

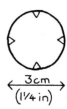

1 *Cut the body and base in white felt, following the measurements shown here. Oversew together the short sides of the body piece, to form the centre back seam, then sew the base evenly round the lower edge, matching the notch marks shown.*

Dumpy angel

2 Turn through to the right side and fit the stiff card circle inside the base, pinning temporarily from the outside. Run a gathering stitch 5mm ($\frac{1}{4}$ in) below the top edge, and stuff the body firmly; leave the gathering thread for the moment.

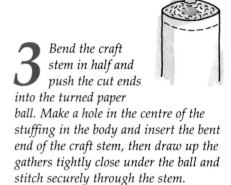

3 Bend the craft stem in half and push the cut ends into the turned paper ball. Make a hole in the centre of the stuffing in the body and insert the bent end of the craft stem, then draw up the gathers tightly close under the ball and stitch securely through the stem.

4 With the right side inside, join the short edges of the dress fabric in a fine seam, press the seam open with your thumbnail, and turn the dress to the right side. Stitch a row of lace half lapping over the lower edge, then another row overlapping the first one. Turn under 5mm ($\frac{1}{4}$ in) round the top and gather close to the edge.

5 Fit the dress on the figure with the join at the back, and draw up tightly around the neck, distributing the gathers evenly. Gather 15cm (6in) of lace and draw up around the neck to form a collar.

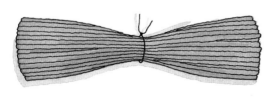

6 For the hair, separate the six strands of embroidery wool and put them together again, to straighten them out. If using knitting yarn, you may need fewer strands. Cut the strands in half, and then into three, each piece thus measuring approximately 13cm (5in). Place them all together and tie the centre loosely with matching thread. Glue over the top of the head as shown in the photograph, to cover the sides and back of the head. Trim the cut ends neatly.

7 *For the halo, overlap the cut ends of the pearl bead trimming and bind the join with thread. Fit it on the head, fastening it with a pin through the join at the back, and gluing the front of the circlet lightly to hold it in place.*

8 *For the cuffs round the hands, gather 10cm (4in) of lace and draw it up to form a rosette, with a 5mm (¼in) hole in the centre. Glue it to the front of the dress, just below the collar. Cut the hands, using the pattern above right, by placing the pattern on the fold of a piece of felt. Oversew the fold to hold the hands together. Glue the fold in the centre of the rosette.*

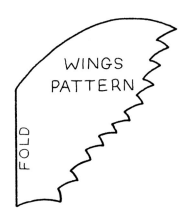

WINGS PATTERN

FOLD

9 *Cut the wings, using the pattern here, by placing the pattern on a piece of folded paper. To transfer the pattern see basics section 5. Open out the wings and with the edge of the fold uppermost, spread glue stick all over this side of both wings. Sprinkle glitter over them, pat it in and shake off the excess.*

10 *When quite dry, fasten the wings with a pin through the fold – to the back of the head near the top of the fold, and to the body near the bottom of the fold.*

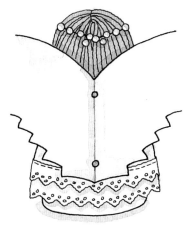

11 *Draw the features, following the face in the photograph for guidance, and fix a 15cm (6in) thread to the top of the head to form a loop.*

Santa

This jolly Father Christmas can be made in next-to-no-time, making him a useful last minute decoration. He measures approximately 11cm (4½in) from the top of his hat to the tip of his beard and his hat is 4.5cm (1¾in) wide at the widest point.

> ## MATERIALS
>
> **Table tennis ball, or a 4cm (1½in) diameter craft ball – for the head.**
>
> **6cm x 10cm (2½in x 4in) of scarlet felt – for the hat.**
>
> **20cm (¼yd) of white velvet tubing ribbon.**
>
> **Polyester filling, or cotton wool – for the beard.**
>
> **Pink wooden bead about 8mm (⁵⁄₁₆in) in diameter – for the nose.**
>
> **15cm (6in) of black thread – for the hanging loop.**
>
> **Scarlet sewing thread (optional).**
>
> **2cm x 4cm (¾in x 1½in) piece of black paper – for the eyes.**
>
> **Flesh poster colour.**
>
> **Clear adhesive.**

1 Make a hole in the ball, push in a wooden skewer or similar object so that it is firmly held, and paint the ball with the flesh poster colour. Allow it to dry thoroughly. Do not take the skewer out of the ball at this stage; leave it in until the head is finished.

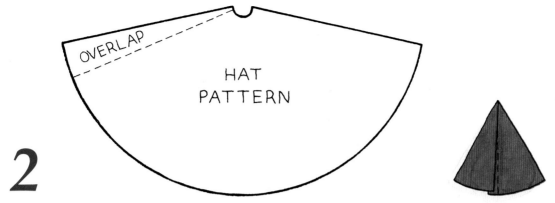

2

Cut out the hat in felt, using this pattern. Curve it round to form a cone and either stitch or glue the overlap.

3 For the bobble on the hat, curve a 2.5cm (1in) length of velvet tubing round into a loop and glue the cut ends together. The join will go at the back; fix the black thread through the front of the circle of tubing, knotting the cut ends underneath, to form a hanging loop. Glue the tip of the hat up into the tubing, to form the bobble on the hat.

4 Glue the hat to the head, then glue velvet tubing around the edge of the felt. Tear off and shape a generous beard of polyester filling or cotton wool; mine was approximately 7cm (2¾in) long and 6cm (2½in) wide. Spread glue over the sides and lower part of the face and press the beard into it.

5 Holding the bead for the nose with tweezers, glue the nose into position against the face and beard. Trace the eye shown here actual size on to thin paper. Fold the black paper in half to make a 2cm (¾in) square, and place the tracing paper on top. Holding the paper tightly at the point marked X on the diagram, cut round the eye shape. Glue the eyes to the face.

Glowing lanterns

Like the hearts earlier, squared paper is the secret of these quick-to-make decorations. My squares were 5mm (³/₁₆in), making a lantern 6.5cm (2¹/₂in) tall, but if you want a bigger lantern use larger squares and adjust the size of the coloured paper and foil accordingly.

A good quality writing paper (see suppliers section at the back of the book) is perfect for this design, in a whole range of colours as well as black.

MATERIALS

Medium-weight black or other coloured paper – one piece 6.5cm x 10cm (2¹/₂in x 4in) for the lantern cylinder, and another piece 9cm x 10cm (3¹/₂in x 4in) for the struts of the lantern.

Red, gold or other coloured foil, 5cm x 10cm (2in x 4in) – for the cylinder of the lantern.

Squared paper.

Piece of plain paper about 15cm (6in) square.

Double sided tape, or all purpose adhesive.

Standard adhesive tape.

15cm (6in) of very narrow satin ribbon – for a hanging loop.

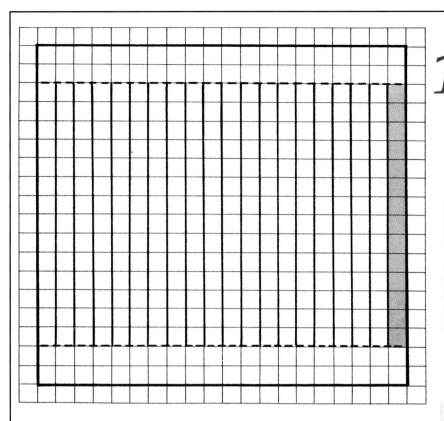

1 *Draw this pattern on squared paper and cut out round the outer edge only.*

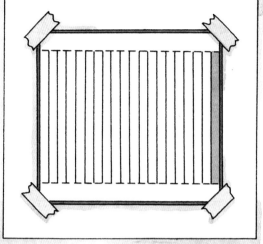

2 *Place the piece of plain paper on a cutting surface, with the larger piece of black paper centrally on top. Place the squared paper pattern over it, edges exactly matching, and tape the corners to hold it in position. Score the horizontal broken lines on the pattern, then cut all the vertical lines with a sharp knife, going through the pattern and the black paper. Cut the tape to release the paper and discard the pattern and backing paper. Re-score and crease the broken lines on the black paper, and cut away the strip shown shaded.*

3 *Roll the smaller piece of black paper into a cylinder and tape a 5mm (¹/₄in) overlap. Wrap the coloured foil around the centre of the tube and tape the overlap.*

4 *Apply double-sided tape around the top and bottom edges of the tube, for a depth of approximately 1cm (³/₈in), trimming off any surplus. Then stick the cut black paper to it around the tube, keeping the top and bottom edges of the black paper exactly level with the edges of the tube. The cut strips of black paper will thus 'balloon out'. Trim off, or glue, the slight overlap of black paper.*

5 *Make two holes opposite each other in the top of the lantern, using a small hole punch or the point of compasses. Fix a loop of the very narrow ribbon across the top, knotting the ends together inside.*

Quilled snowflakes

A few tiny mother-of pearl sequins glued here and there are hardly noticeable, but they glisten like winter frost when the Christmas tree lights are switched on.

The pearl bead set in the centre matches the tiny seed pearls in the surrounding teardrops and in the outer circle of marquises.

Plain white paper, glue and a quilling tool are all you need to make these pretty and inexpensive decorations. Sequins and pearls add shimmer and sparkle.

The snowflakes are made from plain white writing paper and are formed from only three of the standard quilling shapes: teardrops, marquises and circles. The snowflakes can be larger or smaller, simply by including more or fewer shapes. For any of these snowflakes thirty teardrops are needed, some of which are turned into marquises as the design progresses.

MATERIALS

Good quality plain white writing paper.

Pearl or glass beads, sequins, etc – for decoration.

Quilling tool.

Dark green or black sewing thread – for hanging loop.

Adhesives.

Quilling tools are available from art or craft shops, and are not expensive. Or you can make your own version by burying the point of a long, strong darning needle in a cork.

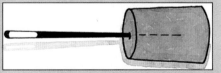

Use either a PVA or an all purpose clear adhesive to stick the shapes. My own preference is PVA to make the shapes themselves, and an all purpose adhesive to join them together, because it dries more quickly. But it is not essential to buy two adhesives; either is perfectly satisfactory for both purposes.

A mother-of-pearl flower sequin, centred with a tiny diamante, is mounted on a loose circle. A few domed sequins, to match the flower sequin, make a shimmering outer circle, placed in the points of the snowflake.

A silver star sequin sparkles at the centre, and the teardrops in the two surrounding circles each have a small white glass bead in the middle.

1 The paper strips used are 3mm (¹/₈in) wide; the length can be varied but I find that about 20cm (8in) is a good average. A 15cm (6in) strip will give a more open, lacy effect, but the snowflake will not be as strong. To cut the strips, prepare a piece of writing paper 20cm (8in) wide and about 12cm (5in) deep. This will give a few extra strips so that any that are not perfect can be discarded. Rule a vertical line 3.5cm (1³/₈in) from one end of the paper, and mark the sides every 3mm (¹/₈in). Cut using a very sharp craft knife and a metal rule, as the strips must be measured and cut very accurately and cleanly. If you are using a card cutting board, renew it frequently because as it becomes scored it will snag the paper. A self-healing cutting mat is ideal.

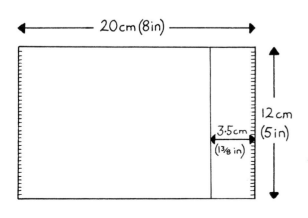

2 Fit into the tip of the quilling tool the end of the strip furthest from the marked line; moisten the paper if it does not hold. Twist the tool between the fingertips as shown by the arrow here, rolling it smoothly and tightly round and round to the end. Release the paper from the tool, allowing it to open a little.

Quilled snowflakes

3 Fit the end of the strip against the marked line and pinch into a teardrop shape, folding at the marked line; glue the tip of the strip so that the cut end is level with the fold. If the end overlaps the fold, snip it level.

4 For a marquise, simply pinch the teardrop at the opposite side as well.

5 For a loose circle, when you have rolled up the strip, glue the end level with the marked line without pinching the shape. To place a bead at the centre of the circle, unroll the strip, spread a little adhesive along about 2cm (³/₄ in) of the paper at the end that is inside the roll, and roll up the strip again with the bead in the centre; then glue the end so that the strip is rolled tightly around the bead.

6 To make the snowflake, trace this pattern in the centre of a 15cm (6in) square or circle of good tracing paper or non-stick cooking parchment, extending all the lines out to the edge. Turn the tracing over so that the pencil lines are underneath and will not smudge the snowflake. If you are having a centre motif in your snowflake place this exactly at the hub of the spokes on the tracing; otherwise use the hub as the centre point of the design.

7 Using tweezers arrange six shapes around the centre, then glue them lightly in position against each other wherever they meet, each one positioned directly over a solid traced line.

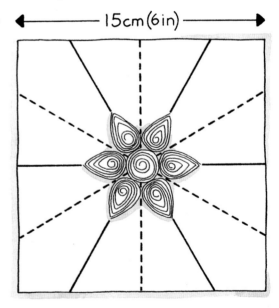

◄─ 15cm (6in) ─►

8 Experiment with the remaining pieces, using the examples of snowflakes on these pages for guidance. Build up the snowflake in any way you please, perhaps adding another circle of six teardrops or marquises between the first ones, setting them over the broken lines on the tracing, and then placing six batches of three teardrops or marquises between those, to form the six branches of the snowflake – see the examples. When assembling the snowflake it is essential always to keep it absolutely flat on the working surface.

9 Using tweezers and PVA adhesive, insert beads in the snowflake or glue sequins on top, as shown in the examples on these pages.

10 When the snowflake is finished leave it to dry thoroughly, then lift the tracing paper and gently peel it off the back. To hang the decoration, fix a loop of black or green thread through one of the shapes at the end of a branch of the snowflake.

Elves and fairies

Sitting on upturned cones, the holly and
mistletoe fairies accompany the ivy leaf and
poinsettia elves. Each decoration, including
the cone, is approximately 11cm (4¼ in) high.

Elves and fairies

The figures are easily made from velvet tubing (see supplier section). For one elf and fairy I used real ivy and holly leaves, but you could make them from double crêpe paper, as I did for the leaves on the other two decorations.

Double crêpe paper (see supplier section) is lovely to use because it is a different shade on the reverse; but if you do not have any you can stick two pieces of single crêpe paper together with dry stick adhesive.

MATERIALS

25cm (10in) of Offray velvet tubing in one colour for the basic figure; or when using two colours, 14cm (5½in) for the body and arms, and 10cm (4in) for the legs.

Two pipe cleaners or chenille stems, 15cm (6in) long – for the 'skeleton' of the figures.

Flesh-tinted turned paper craft ball 3cm (1¼in) in diameter – for the head.

Two natural wood beads, 8-10mm in diameter – for the hands.

Two coloured wood beads, 8-10mm in diameter – for the feet.

Twilleys stranded embroidery wool, or fine knitting yarn – six 76cm (30in) strands for an elf's hair, and nine 76cm (30in) strands for a fairy.

25cm (10in) of 2cm (¾in) wide lace – for a fairy's tutu.

30cm (12in) of 1cm (⅜in) wide lace – for a fairy's neck and wrist frills.

15cm (6in) of 1cm (⅜in) wide lace – for an elf's neck frill.

Medium pearl beads – for the mistletoe fairy's circlet.

Tiny red beads – for the holly fairy's hat.

Small gold bead – for the poinsettia elf's cap.

Natural leaves or double crêpe paper or stiff medium-weight coloured paper, in green and red – for wings and caps.

Sepia watercolour crayon or standard crayon, or ballpoint pen – for drawing features.

Sewing thread in black and colour(s) to match velvet tubing.

Fir cone, about 5cm (2in) high.

Pins.

Clear adhesive.

The mistletoe fairy is made in all white velvet tubing.

The ivyleaf fairy has all emerald velvet tubing.

The holly fairy has a scarlet top and black legs.

The poinsettia elf has a black top and scarlet legs.

---

1 Cut the pipe cleaners or chenille stems, and the velvet tubing, as follows:

	Pipe cleaner	Velvet tubing
Arms	8.5cm (3½in)	8.5cm (3½in)
Body	6.5cm (2½in)	5.5cm (2in)
(use remainder of arms pipe cleaner)		
Legs	11cm (4¼in)	11cm (4¼in)

2 Push the pieces of pipe cleaner or chenille stem through the tubing so that they protrude equally at each end; hold the inner cord of the velvet tubing to prevent it slipping, but if it does move don't worry, just pull it out and discard it. Bend the body in half and glue the arms between; mark the centre of the arms with a pin to ensure the arms are exactly equal. Bend the legs as shown here, then stitch the body and legs securely together. Glue on the appropriate beads for the hands and feet.

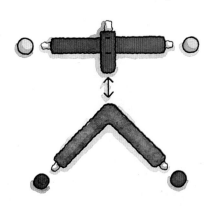

3 Examine the turned paper ball to choose the best surface for the face; indicate this with a pencil arrow on top of the head. Then glue the ball on to the ends of the body pipe cleaner or stem.

4 *To dress either fairy, join the cut ends of the tutu lace, then gather the straight edge and draw it up tightly round the waist, distributing the gathers evenly. Cut the narrower lace in half and gather one half for the neck frill, drawing it up and distributing the gathers round the neck. Join at the neck. Cut the other half in half again, and gather each piece along the centre for the wrist frills. Draw up round the wrists and secure. To dress either elf, gather the lace round the neck as for the fairies.*

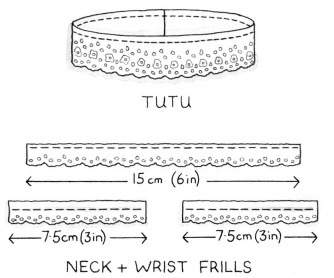

TUTU

NECK + WRIST FRILLS

15 cm (6 in)

7.5 cm (3 in)   7.5 cm (3 in)

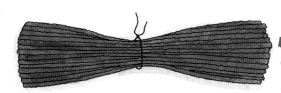

5 *For the fairies' hair, separate nine strands of embroidery wool, then put them together again and cut them in half. If you are using knitting wool you may need fewer strands. Tie the centre loosely with a single strand, then glue the tied area on top of the head, spreading the strands out evenly all round the sides and back, and gluing them into place. Trim the cut ends neatly to length.*

6 *For the elves' hair, separate six strands of embroidery wool, then put them together again and cut them in half three times. If you are using knitting yarn you may need fewer strands. Tie the centre tightly with a single strand, then glue the tied area to the crown and spread the strands out evenly all round. Trim to length, following the photographs for guidance.*

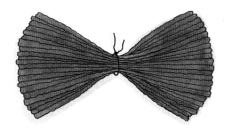

7 *To complete the holly fairy, pin holly leaves to her back for wings, or use a holly leaf to make a template and cut the leaves in crêpe or thick paper. Cut away the bottom of a smaller leaf, rounding off the base as shown here, and glue it to the top of her head. Thread a 2.5cm (1in) length of tiny red beads and tie to form a circle. Glue on top of the leaf.*

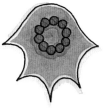

8 *To complete the mistletoe fairy, trace this leaf pattern and make a template (basics section 5) for the wings. Cut out two in crêpe or thick paper and pin them to her back. Thread a 6cm (2½in) length of pearl beads and tie to form a circle. Glue it to the top of the head.*

WING
PATTERN

9 To complete the ivy leaf elf, pin ivy leaves to his back for wings, or use an ivy leaf to make a template and cut out the leaves in crêpe or thick paper. Glue a tiny leaf to the top of the head for his hat, or make one from paper.

10 To complete the poinsettia elf, trace the leaf pattern given here and make a template (basics section 5) for the wings. Cut out two in crêpe or thick paper and pin them to his back. Use the patterns here to make templates for the flower and cut out five petals in red crêpe paper or alternative, and one circle. Glue the petals evenly round on top of the circle, then glue it to the top of his head and pin or glue the gold bead at the centre.

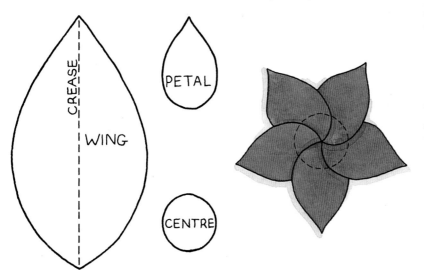

11 For facial features of all of the figures, mark round dots for the eyes, with a tiny line between them for the nose, and draw a curve for the mouth, as shown in the photograph.

12 To assemble each decoration, bend the figure into a sitting position on the upturned cone, then spread a blob of glue over the figure's seat and another over the spot on the cone where it will sit. Allow the glue to become tacky, then press the figure and cone firmly together. To keep the figure sitting upright, push a tiny pin down the base of its back and into the cone. The pin will not penetrate very far, but it will be enough to hold the figure in position.

13 To attach a hanging loop, thread a needle with a 20cm (8in) length of black thread and push it right through the head, from side to side, avoiding hats, caps etc. Knot the ends, forming a loop to hang.

1. Ribbon roses

Ideally use a single-face satin ribbon for roses, except for the 3mm (1/8in) ribbon, which comes only in double-face satin. This 3mm (1/8in) ribbon makes a miniature rose and it is sensible to become familiar with the technique before attempting it, as it is a little fiddly.

Choose a suitable colour; the Offray range of ribbons used on the projects in this book offers a wide choice of realistic shades that are as close as you can get to nature. On the other hand, unnatural colours can look just as attractive in certain situations. Sable brown roses on a cream background, for instance, can look stunning, as can mauve or blue.

1 Cut off the required amount of ribbon; this will depend on the number of petals wanted but the following is a good average:

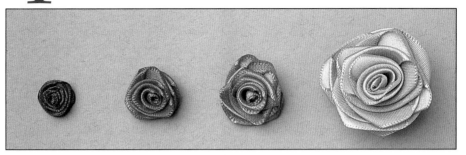

Width of ribbon
3mm (1/8in)
Length required
11cm (4 1/2in)

Width of ribbon
7mm (1/4in)
Length required
15cm (6in)

Width of ribbon
9mm (3/8in)
Length required
20cm (8in)

Width of ribbon
15mm (5/8in)
Length required
30-40cm (12-16in)

2 Fold the corner over, as shown by the broken line, bringing point A down to meet point B.

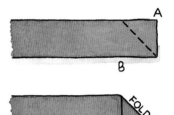

3 Bring point C over to meet points A and B.

4 Roll the ribbon around three or four times, with the folded corner inside, to form a tight tube, and make a few holding stitches through the base.

5 To make the petal, fold the ribbon down so that the edge is aligned with the tube. Then curve the ribbon around the tube to form a cone, keeping the top of the tube level with the diagonal fold.

6 When the tube again lies parallel with the remaining ribbon, take a couple of stitches through the base to hold the petal you have just made.

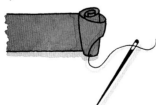

7 Continue to make petals with the remainder of the ribbon, sewing each one to the base of the flower before starting the next.

8 Shape the rose as you work by gradually making the petals a little more open. Finish with the cut end tucked neatly underneath the base of the completed rose.

2. Plaited braid

Use 1.5mm (¹/₁₆in) wide satin ribbon. To estimate the amount you will need, measure the length of braid that you require, add a third of that length, and then multiply the result by three. For example, for a 15cm (6in) length of braid you will require:

15cm + 5cm (6in + 2in) = 20cm (8in)
x 3 = 60cm (24in)

If you want to make a multicoloured braid, calculate the amount of each colour separately, ie not multiplying by three. In the above example this would mean 20cm of each of three colours.

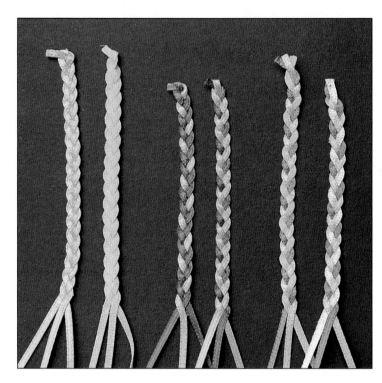

Each braid in one colour — Each braid in two colours — Multicoloured braid with three colours

1 *When using ribbon of one colour, fold the ribbon into three, but cut only one fold. Glue one end of the shorter piece inside the fold of the longer piece, and pinch together. Glue in the same way if using two colours, as shown here. If making a multicoloured braid, just glue all three cut ends together.*

2 *Push a pin through the glued end and secure it to a drawing board or something similar. Then begin to plait very evenly, making sure that the strands of ribbon are always flat; never fold them over. Keep the ribbon taut, and draw the plait very firmly between the fingertips every 2-3cm (an inch or so) to make it smooth and even. Hold the ends together with a paper clip.*

3 *Glue the braid into place, spreading the glue on the braid just beyond the point where you intend to cut it, to ensure that it does not unravel. Press the cut ends down well, adding a little more glue if necessary.*

3. Butterfly bows

Width of ribbon 1.5mm ($^1/_{16}$ in) Length required 6cm ($2^1/_2$ in)	Width of ribbon 3mm ($^1/_8$ in) Length required 8cm ($3^1/_4$ in)	Width of ribbon 7mm ($^1/_4$ in) Length required 10cm (4in)	Width of ribbon 9mm ($^3/_8$ in) Length required 12.5cm (5in)	Width of ribbon 15mm ($^5/_8$ in) Length required 15cm (6in)

Use single-face or double-face satin ribbon. All the measurements for these bows are variable, so the length required will depend on the ribbon width, the effect you wish to create, and the length you want the streamers to be.

Experience and experimentation will determine your own personal preferences, but the examples given above are a good average to work on for a standard shaped bow made from the narrower ribbon widths.

With a very wide ribbon the directions differ slightly – see the instructions for the stocking sachets elsewhere in the book.

1 On the wrong (dull) side of the ribbon, mark point A at the centre, close to the lower edge as shown here. Mark points B and C equally either side of the centre, close to the top edge. Cut the ends in an inverted V-shape, or do this afterwards if you prefer – and don't do it at all for the narrowest ribbons.

2 Hold the ribbon with the wrong side facing you. Using matching thread, bring the needle through point A from the back. Then curve the left end round and bring the needle through point B; curve the right end round and bring the needle through point C. Draw up the thread so that B and C are on top of A.

3 Take the needle up and through the centre top of the back length of the ribbon – marked D on the drawing. Then take it down at the back and bring it through to the front again to emerge at point E on the drawing.

4 Take the thread up and over the top and wrap it tightly round the middle several times, drawing up and shaping the bow as you do so. Finish off neatly and securely at the back.

4. Blowing an egg

1 Make small holes at each end of the egg with a darning needle, the hole at the rounded end of the egg slightly larger than the other; begin by gently scratching the surface before finally breaking through the shell, and then enlarge the hole to the required size with the point of the needle.

When emptied of their contents ordinary hen's eggs are so light they are ideal for hanging from the tree as decorations. Pasting the outside with a covering of papier mâché, as for the baubles in this book, gives the delicate shell strength or resilience. Make sure that you clean out the egg thoroughly before you start, and that no remnants of egg yolk remain inside, to avoid any unpleasant smells later!

2 Push the needle inside and gently stir it around to break up the yolk and mix it with the white.

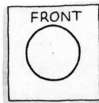

3 Holding the egg over a basin, blow through the hole at the pointed end until the shell is empty.

4 Wash the eggshell very thoroughly in detergent, inside and out. Then set it, pointed end up, in an egg-cup until thoroughly dry; a cool oven hurries things along, and ensures no moisture remains inside.

5. Transferring a tracing and making a template

When you need to reproduce the outline of a pattern from the book on to a surface you cannot see through, such as thick paper or card, trace it off and transfer it as described here.

1 Trace the outline of the pattern from the book on to household greaseproof paper.

FRONT

2 Turn the paper over and rub over the back of the outline with a soft pencil.

BACK

3 Turn the paper back to the front again and fix it securely to the surface to which the tracing is to be transferred. Then draw over the outline again with a firm point, such as a ballpoint pen, hard pencil or knitting needle.

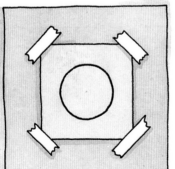

4 When the tracing paper is removed, a clear outline should remain. If necessary, clean up the paper around it with an eraser.

5 **To make a template** transfer the tracing of the outline as described above on to stiff paper, or thin card if extra rigidity is required. Cut it out and use this as a pattern round which to cut your crêpe paper, fabric etc.